J 743.6977 BERGIN
J 743.6977 BERGIN
Bergin, Mark,
Draw dogs & puppies /
33341007962649

14+7/23 W

STEP-BY-STEP™

DRAW

DOGS

& PUPPIES

MARK BERGIN

BOOK HOUSE

This edition first published in MMXVII by
Book House

Distributed by Black Rabbit Books
P.O. Box 3263
Mankato
Minnesota MN 56002

Cataloging-in-Publication Data is available
from the Library of Congress

Printed in the United States
At Corporate Graphics,
North Mankato, Minnesota

9 8 7 6 5 4 3 2 1

ISBN: 978-1-911242-22-2

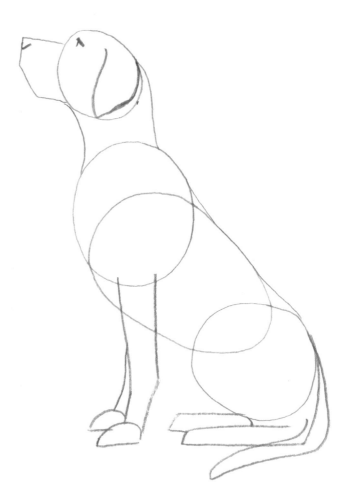

CONTENTS

MAKING A START

Learning to draw is about looking and seeing. Keep practicing and get to know your subject. Use a sketchbook to make quick drawings. Start by doodling, and experiment with shapes and patterns. There are many ways to draw; this book shows only some methods. Visit art galleries, look at artists' drawings, see how friends draw, but above all, find your own way.

Sketch dogs in everyday surroundings. This will help you to draw faster and to capture the main elements of a pose quickly.

4

Starting with basic construction lines can help
you when drawing different dog positions.

There are many different breeds of dog to
draw. Use a sketchbook to draw as many types
of dog as you can find.

The only way to get
better is to keep
practicing. If a drawing
looks wrong, start again.
Keep working at it.

DRAWING MATERIALS

Try using different types of drawing paper and materials. Experiment with charcoal, wax crayons, and pastels. All pens, from felt-tips to ballpoints, will make interesting marks— you could also try drawing with pen and ink on wet paper.

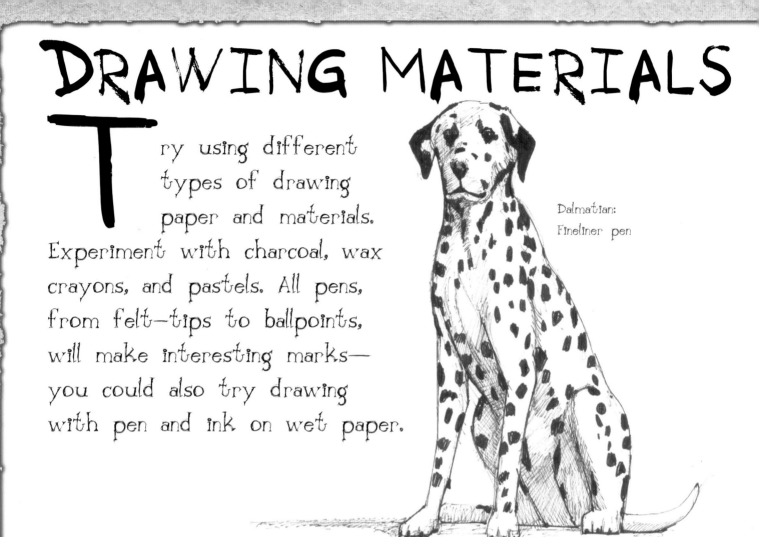

Dalmatian: Fineliner pen

Silhouette is a style of drawing that uses only a solid black shape.

It can be tricky adding light and shade with an **ink pen**. Analyze your drawing. The lightest areas should be left untouched. Then apply solid areas of ink to the darkest parts. The midtones are achieved by hatching (single parallel lines) or cross-hatching (criss-crossed lines).

Ink silhouette

Lines drawn in **ink** cannot be erased, so keep your ink drawings sketchy and less rigid. Don't worry about mistakes as these lines can be lost in the drawing as it develops.

Beagle: Colored pencil

Felt—tips come in a range of line widths. The broader tips are good for filling in large areas of flat tone.

Hard pencils are grayer and soft pencils are blacker. Hard pencils are usually graded from 6H (the hardest) through 5H, 4H, 3H, and 2H to H.

Yorkshire Terrier: Felt—tip pen

Soft pencils are graded from B, 2B, 3B, 4B, and 5B up to 6B (the softest).

Schnauzer: Pencil

7

PERSPECTIVE

If you look at any object from different viewpoints, you will see that the part that is closest to you looks larger, and the part furthest away from you looks smaller. Drawing in perspective is a way of creating a feeling of depth— of showing three dimensions on a flat surface.

German Pointer

The vanishing point (V.P.) is the place in a perspective drawing where parallel lines appear to meet. The position of the vanishing point depends on the viewer's eye level. Sometimes an unusually high or low viewpoint can give your drawing added drama.

Low eye level (view from below)

V.P. = vanishing point

V.P.

Dalmatian

V.P.

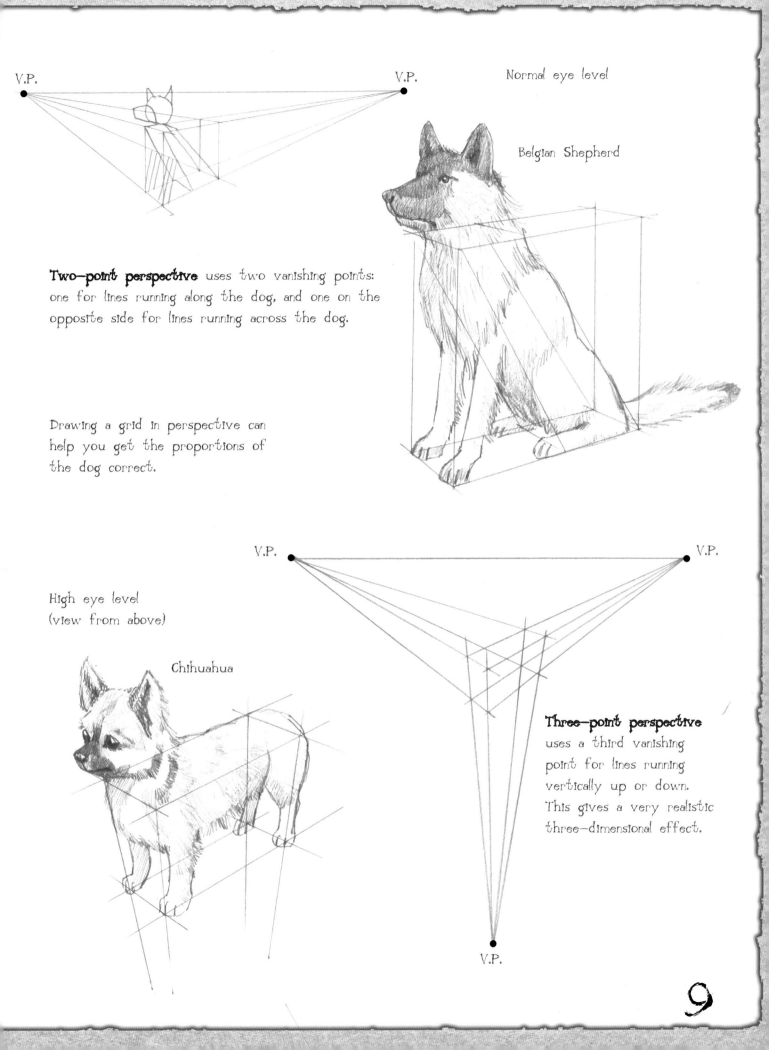

V.P.   V.P.

Normal eye level

Belgian Shepherd

Two-point perspective uses two vanishing points: one for lines running along the dog, and one on the opposite side for lines running across the dog.

Drawing a grid in perspective can help you get the proportions of the dog correct.

High eye level
(view from above)

Chihuahua

V.P.   V.P.

Three-point perspective uses a third vanishing point for lines running vertically up or down. This gives a very realistic three-dimensional effect.

V.P.

9

SIMPLE SHAPES

By using circles and simple shapes you can explore different poses. Each dog has its own way of sitting, walking, or running, and with practice you can learn to capture these quickly.

Draw circular shapes for the main features of the dog: the head, shoulders, hips, knees, and feet.

Draw in lines to connect these main sections to create the shape of the dog.

The line of the spine helps to ensure that all parts are correctly aligned.

11

BASIC ANATOMY

These side view drawings of dogs show their underlying muscle structure. The small drawings show that the dogs' main muscle groups just under the skin are in the same formation whatever the shape and size of the dog breed.

Australian Cattle Dog

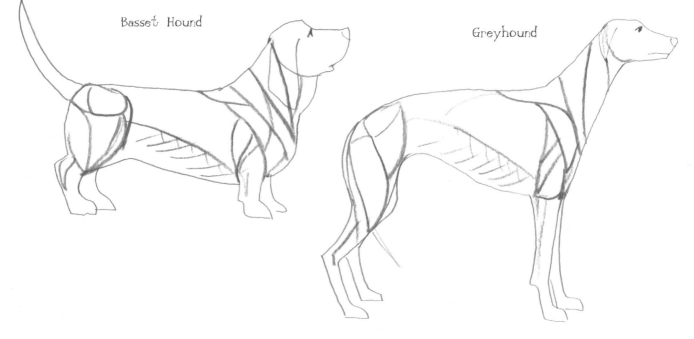

Basset Hound

Greyhound

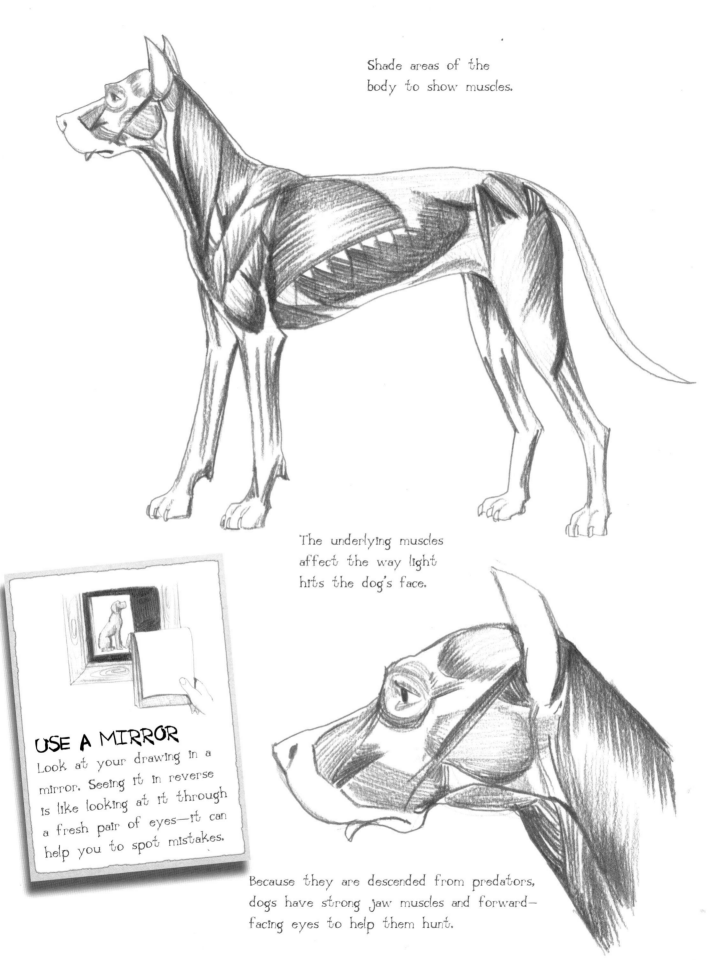

Shade areas of the
body to show muscles.

The underlying muscles
affect the way light
hits the dog's face.

USE A MIRROR
Look at your drawing in a
mirror. Seeing it in reverse
is like looking at it through
a fresh pair of eyes—it can
help you to spot mistakes.

Because they are descended from predators,
dogs have strong jaw muscles and forward-
facing eyes to help them hunt.

PAWS, TAILS, NOSES, AND EARS

Studying and sketching the detailed features will help you with your final drawings. It's important to get these features right because they add character.

Quick pencil sketches can help you to understand the structure of paws and claws. Look for areas where tone should be darker and also changes of texture.

Pomeranian   Beagle   Basenji   Airedale Terrier   Toy Poodle   Pug   Siberian Husky   Dalmatian   Akita

Irish Setter   Husky   Pug

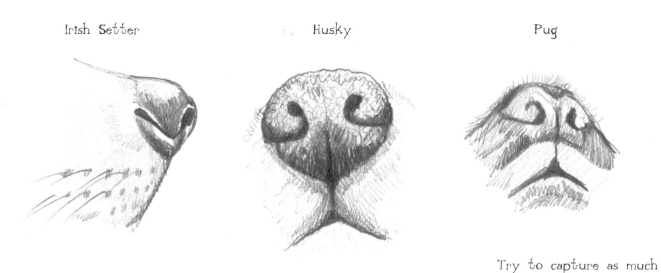

Try to capture as much detail as you can in your sketches.

The more you study a subject and practice drawing it, the more accurate your drawings will become.

Drawing from life and references will help you practice the different parts of a specific breed of dog. The details will make your picture more effective overall.

The different shapes of dogs' ears have names. These are some examples:

Cocked ear   V-shaped ear   Rose ear   Drop ear

Prick ear   Button ear   Folded ear   Cropped ear

15

USING PHOTOS

Drawing from photographs can help you identify shape and form and will help you to draw more accurately.

Choose a good photograph of a dog and trace it.

Pointer

Mark out a grid over your traced drawing. This will divide your drawing into small sections.

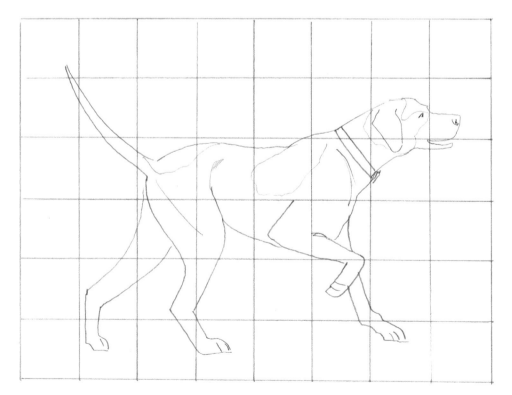

Draw a faint grid of the same proportions on your drawing paper. You can now transfer the shapes from each square of the tracing paper to your drawing paper.

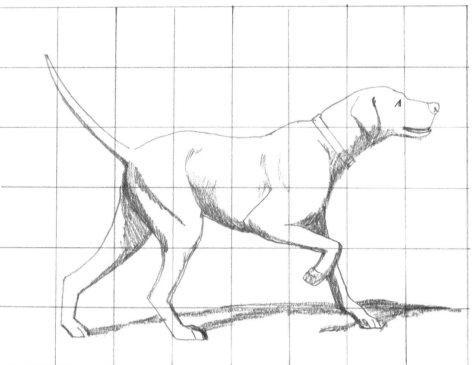

Light source

To make your drawing look three-dimensional, decide which side the light source is coming from, and put in areas of shadow where the light doesn't reach.

Sketch in an overall tone and add surrounding textures to create interest and a sense of movement. Pay attention to the position of your drawing on the paper—this is called composition.

17

DRAWING HEADS

P ractice drawing the shape of dogs' heads, either from real life or photographs. Dogs' heads come in so many shapes and sizes depending on the breed. Look carefully as the shape can be quite distinctive.

Labrador

Use basic construction lines to build up the particular shape of the dog's head.

Cardigan Welsh Corgi

Boxer

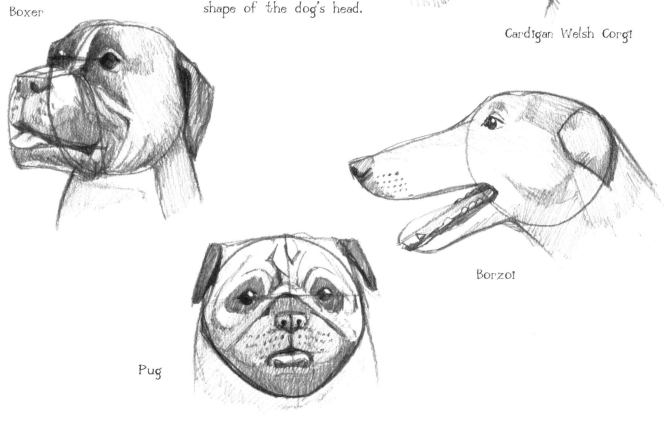

Borzoi

Pug

Leave a white highlight in the eyes to make them look bright and healthy.

Beagle

Once you have drawn the basic shape of the dog's face, add more detail with shading.

Remove any unwanted construction lines with an eraser.

Labrador puppy

PUPPY POSES

Drawing a puppy from observation will help you to capture its natural pose and movement. This will create a dynamic and lifelike drawing.

Use short pencil strokes for fur, and sketch any distinctive markings.

Think about which direction the light is coming from and use shading for areas that the light doesn't reach. This makes the drawing look three-dimensional.

BORDER COLLIE

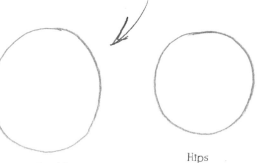

Border Collie dogs were originally bred to herd sheep. They are hardworking, energetic, and fun, and are considered one of the most intelligent dog breeds.

Draw two circles, the larger one for the top of the shoulders and the other for the top of the hips.

Shoulders   Hips

Draw another circle for the head.

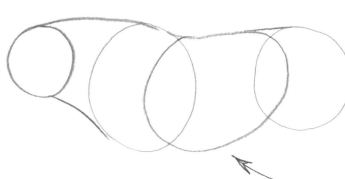

Join the circles with simple lines and an oval shape for the body.

Sketch the basic shape of the hind legs. Note how the thigh curves gracefully into the hip.

Sketch in the shape of the front legs and paws.

22

Add pointed shapes for the ears.

Add the shape of the tail.

Sketch in construction lines to place the dog's muzzle.

Add details to the dog's face: eyes, nose, teeth, and tongue.

Sketch in darker areas of fur to help define the shape of the dog's muscles.

Add lines to the feet to define the paws.

Complete the details of the head.

Add areas of short lines to create the fur texture on the dog's body.

Remove any unwanted construction lines with an eraser.

23

BEARDED COLLIE

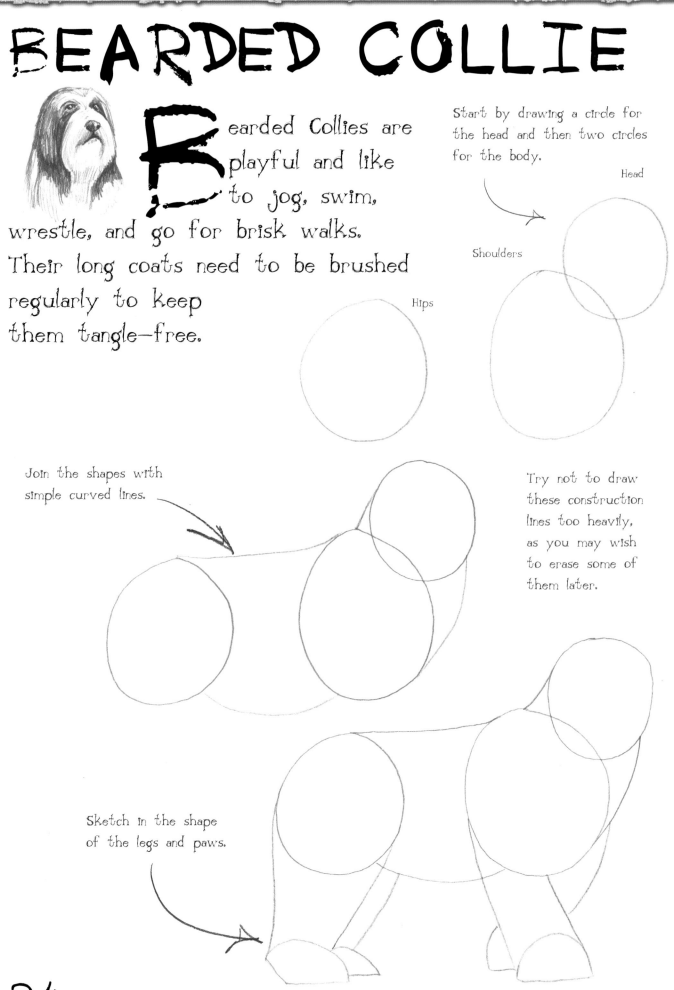

Bearded Collies are playful and like to jog, swim, wrestle, and go for brisk walks. Their long coats need to be brushed regularly to keep them tangle-free.

Start by drawing a circle for the head and then two circles for the body.

Head

Shoulders

Hips

Join the shapes with simple curved lines.

Try not to draw these construction lines too heavily, as you may wish to erase some of them later.

Sketch in the shape of the legs and paws.

Draw a curved
shape for the ear.

Sketch in the dog's muzzle along
with the eyes, nose, and mouth.

Add lines to the feet
to define the paws.

Add a line for the tail
and a wavy line for
the fur on the body.

Add more detail
to the dog's face.

Start to add fur
to the body with
shading.

Shade the dog's body, but remember
to leave some light areas for the
Collie's distinctive markings.

Draw jagged lines around the lower
edges of the dog's body to create
the Bearded Collie's long fur.

25

SIBERIAN HUSKY

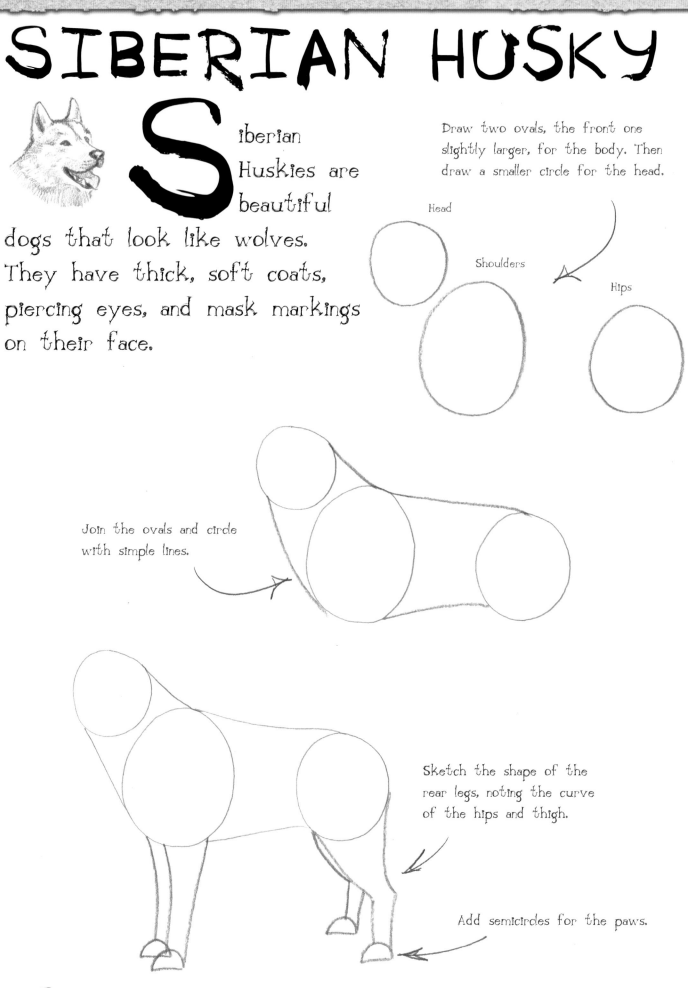

Siberian Huskies are beautiful dogs that look like wolves. They have thick, soft coats, piercing eyes, and mask markings on their face.

Draw two ovals, the front one slightly larger, for the body. Then draw a smaller circle for the head.

Head

Shoulders

Hips

Join the ovals and circle with simple lines.

Sketch the shape of the rear legs, noting the curve of the hips and thigh.

Add semicircles for the paws.

Draw the dog's open
mouth and sketch the
shape of its tongue.

Add two pointed shapes
for the dog's ears.

Draw in
the tail.

Add detail to the
face. Sketch in the
eyes and nose.

Begin to add shading to the dog's
body to emphasize the muscles.

Add shade to areas where
light wouldn't reach.

Finish adding shading and
tone to add texture
to the dog's coat.

Complete all details of
the head and markings.

Remove any unwanted
construction lines.

27

SITTING WEIMARANER

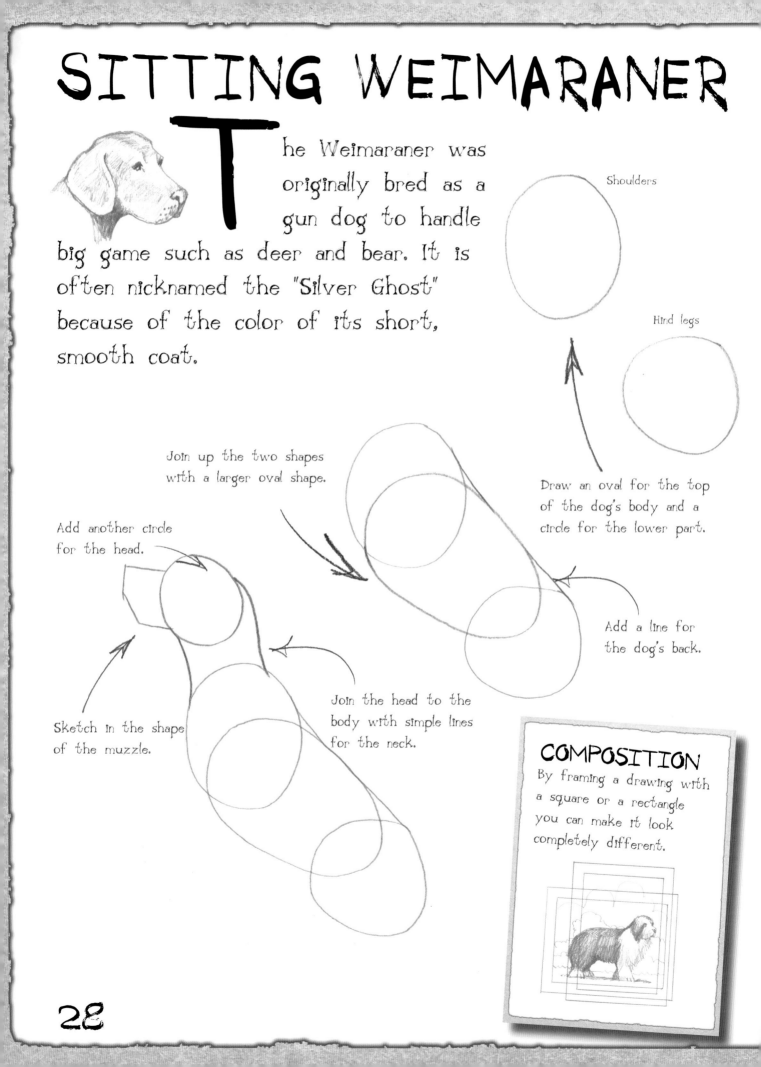

The Weimaraner was originally bred as a gun dog to handle big game such as deer and bear. It is often nicknamed the "Silver Ghost" because of the color of its short, smooth coat.

Shoulders

Hind legs

Draw an oval for the top of the dog's body and a circle for the lower part.

Join up the two shapes with a larger oval shape.

Add another circle for the head.

Add a line for the dog's back.

Join the head to the body with simple lines for the neck.

Sketch in the shape of the muzzle.

COMPOSITION
By framing a drawing with a square or a rectangle you can make it look completely different.

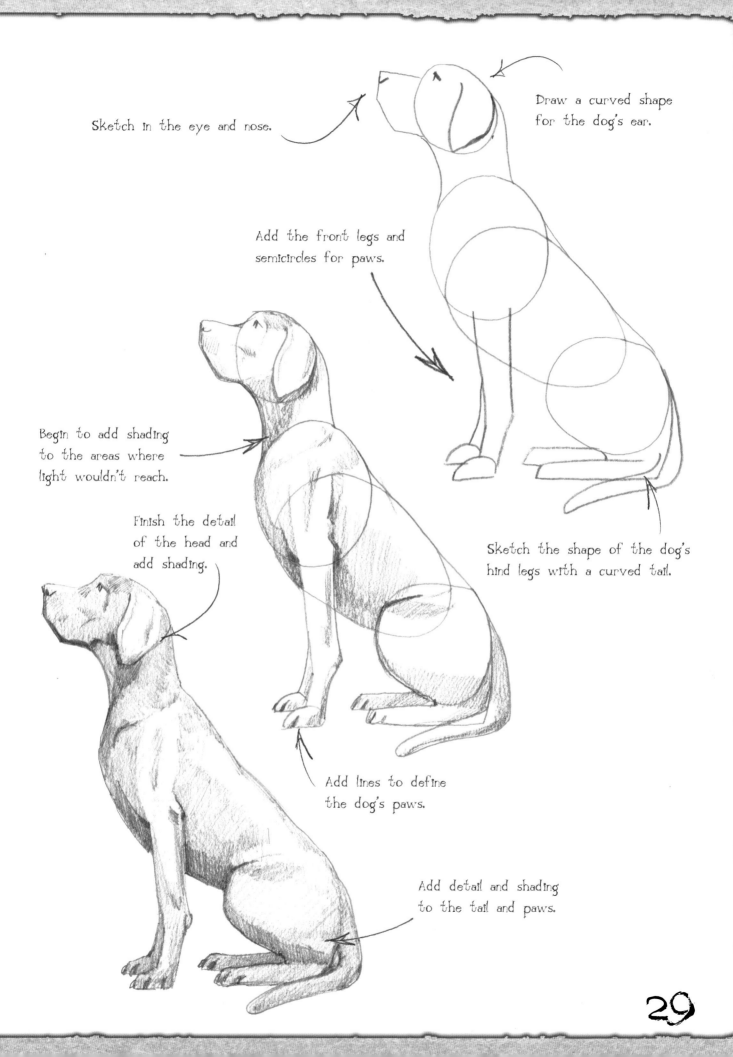

Sketch in the eye and nose.

Draw a curved shape for the dog's ear.

Add the front legs and semicircles for paws.

Begin to add shading to the areas where light wouldn't reach.

Finish the detail of the head and add shading.

Sketch the shape of the dog's hind legs with a curved tail.

Add lines to define the dog's paws.

Add detail and shading to the tail and paws.

29

DOG AND PUPPIES

Some dogs may give birth to a single puppy, but other breeds can carry up to 17 puppies in a single litter!

Start by drawing three circles and joining them with two simple lines.

For the front legs draw tube shapes with curved paws.

Draw curved ears and sketch the shape of the dog's muzzle.

Draw rounded shapes for the hind paws with simple lines creating the legs.

Sketch curved lines for the tail.

Start to add detail to the paws.

Draw the construction lines for the two puppies using the same basic shapes as before.

Begin to add detail to the faces with eyes and noses.

Think about which direction the light is coming from and shade any areas it wouldn't reach.

Use short lines to create a fluffy tail.

Add tone and shading to the puppies.

31

GLOSSARY

Composition The arrangement of the parts of a picture on the drawing paper.

Construction lines Guidelines used in the early stages of a drawing, and usually erased later.

Fixative A kind of resin sprayed over a drawing to prevent smudging. **It should only be used by an adult.**

Light source The direction from which the light seems to come in a drawing.

Perspective A method of drawing in which near objects are shown larger than faraway objects to give an impression of depth.

Pose The position assumed by a figure.

Predator An animal that lives by preying on other animals.

Proportion The correct relationship of scale between each part of the drawing.

Silhouette A drawing that shows only a flat dark shape, like a shadow.

Vanishing point The place in a perspective drawing where parallel lines appear to meet.

INDEX